Unlocking the Secrets of Science

Profiling 20th Century Achievers in Science, Medicine, and Technology

Edwin Hubble and the Theory of the Expanding Universe

Susan Zannos

PO Box 196 • Hockessin, Delaware 19707
www.mitchelllane.com

Unlocking the Secrets of Science

Profiling 20th Century Achievers in Science, Medicine, and Technology

Luis Alvarez and the Development of the Bubble Chamber
Marc Andreessen and the Development of the Web Browser
Oswald Avery and the Story of DNA
Frederick Banting and the Discovery of Insulin
Christiaan Barnard and the Story of the First Successful Heart Transplant
Tim Berners-Lee and the Development of the World Wide Web
Chester Carlson and the Development of Xerography
Wallace Carothers and the Story of DuPont Nylon
Francis Crick and James Watson: Pioneers in DNA Research
Jacques-Yves Cousteau: His Story Under the Sea
Raymond Damadian and the Development of the MRI
Gerhard Domagk and the Discovery of Sulfa
Paul Ehrlich and Modern Drug Development
Albert Einstein and the Theory of Relativity
Willem Einthoven and the Story of Electrocardiography
Philo T. Farnsworth: The Life of Television's Forgotten Inventor
Enrico Fermi and the Nuclear Reactor
Alexander Fleming and the Story of Penicillin
Henry Ford and the Assembly Line
Robert Goddard and the Liquid Rocket Engine
Otto Hahn and the Story of Nuclear Fission
William Hewlett: Pioneer of the Computer Age
Godfrey Hounsfield and the Invention of CAT Scans
Edwin Hubble and the Theory of the Expanding Universe
Robert Jarvik and the First Artificial Heart
Willem Kolff and the Invention of the Dialysis Machine
Barbara McClintock: Pioneering Geneticist
Lise Meitner and the Atomic Age
Joseph E. Murray and the Story of the First Human Kidney Transplant
Linus Pauling and the Chemical Bond
John R. Pierce: Pioneer in Satellite Communications
Charles Richter and the Story of the Richter Scale
Sally Ride: The Story of the First American Female in Space
Edward Roberts and the Story of the Personal Computer
Wilhelm Roentgen and the Discovery of X Rays
Jonas Salk and the Polio Vaccine
Edward Teller and the Development of the Hydrogen Bomb
Selman Waksman and the Discovery of Streptomycin
Robert A. Weinberg and the Search for the Cause of Cancer
Stephen Wozniak and the Story of Apple Computer

Unlocking the Secrets of Science

Profiling 20th Century Achievers in Science, Medicine, and Technology

Edwin Hubble and the Theory of the Expanding Universe

Printing 1 2 3 4 5 6 7 8 9 10

Library of Congress Cataloging-in-Publication Data

Zannos, Susan.

Edwin Hubble and the theory of the expanding universe / Susan Zannos.

p. cm. — (Unlocking the secrets of science)

Summary: Examines the life and accomplishments of astronomer Edwin Hubble, whose discoveries about the nature and size of the universe solved four central problems in cosmology, one of which formed the basis of the "Big Bang Theory."

Includes bibliographical references and index.

ISBN 1-58415-174-9

1. Hubble, Edwin Powell, 1889-1953—Juvenile literature. 2. Astronomers—United States—Biography—Juvenile literature. [1. Hubble, Edwin Powell, 1889-1953. 2. Astronomers.] I. Title. II. Series.

QB36.H83 Z36 2002

520'.92—dc21 2002008335

ABOUT THE AUTHOR: Susan Zannos has been a lifelong educator, having taught at all levels, from preschool to college, in Mexico, Greece, Italy, Russia, and Lithuania, as well as in the United States. She has published a mystery *Trust the Liar* (Walker and Co.) and *Human Types: Essence and the Enneagram* (Samuel Weiser). Her book, *Human Types*, was recently translated into Russian, and in 2003 Susan was invited to tour Russia and lecture about her book. Another book she recently completed, *Careers in Education* (Mitchell Lane), was selected for inclusion in the New York Public Library's "Books for the Teen Age 2003 List." She has written nearly twenty books for children and young adults, including *Chester Carlson and the Development of Xerography* and *The Life and Times of Franz Joseph Haydn* (Mitchell Lane). When not traveling, Susan lives in the Sierra Foothills of Northern California.

PHOTO CREDITS: cover: Carnegie Institution of Washington; pp. 6, 22, 28, 34, 43 Carnegie Institution; p. 9 SuperStock; pp. 12, 17, 18 Jack Roberts

PUBLISHER'S NOTE: This story has been thoroughly researched, and to the best of our knowledge, represents a true story. Documentation of research done for this story can be found on p. 46. Much of this book was written from Hubble's original papers and correspondence, housed at the California Institute of Technology in San Marino, California.

In selecting those persons to be profiled in this series, we first attempted to identify the most notable accomplishments of the 20th century in science, medicine, and technology. When we were done, we noted a serious deficiency in the inclusion of women. For the greater part of the 20th century science, medicine, and technology were male-dominated fields. In many cases, the contributions of women went unrecognized. Women have tried for years to be included in these areas, and in many cases, women worked side by side with men who took credit for their ideas and discoveries. Even as we move forward into the 21st century, we find women still sadly underrepresented. It is not an oversight, therefore, that we profiled mostly male achievers. Information simply does not exist to include a fair selection of women.

Contents

Edwin Hubble irritated many of his fellow astronomers with his arrogant manner, his phony English accent, and his imitation of English habits such as pipe smoking. But in spite of his efforts to impress people with his importance, he was a careful and painstaking scientist whose discoveries completely changed our understanding of the universe. He was the first astronomer to prove that many nebulae were not objects within our Milky Way Galaxy, but were themselves immense galaxies hurtling through space at enormous distances.

Chapter 1

Telescopes

In 1897, John and Jennie Hubble of Marshfield, Missouri asked their son what he wanted for his eighth birthday. They were dismayed when he said that all he wanted was to stay out all night and look at the stars through the telescope that his grandfather had built in his backyard.

Since the boy's birthday was late in November, his parents tried to convince him that he would get too cold. When he promised to dress warmly, they said he would be too tired for school the next day. When he swore that he would be at school on time and do his lessons well, they gave in, confident that the child would soon tire of the dark and cold and come into the house to bed.

They were wrong.

The boy was Edwin Powell Hubble. That long cold November night he spent looking at the brilliant stars through his grandfather's telescope was the first of many, many long cold nights he would spend looking at the stars through telescopes. He would become the Twentieth Century's most famous astronomer and make discoveries that would change human understanding about the nature and size of the universe.

Increasing knowledge about the universe has depended primarily on the development of telescopes. In the ancient world, in countries such as Egypt, China, Babylonia and Greece, astronomers carefully observed the night skies. They figured out many things about the movements of planets and stars. But these early scientists had no telescopes. They had to depend on what their eyes told them. Their eyes told them that the earth was the center of the universe.

They could clearly see that the sun revolved around the earth. The sun came up in the morning in the east, crossed the sky, and went down in the west. The next morning it would reappear in the east. The stars also revolved around the earth. So did the planets, although it required complicated explanations to describe their motions.

Ptolemy, a Greek astronomer who lived during the second century AD, did a thorough job of describing in detail the motions of the sun and planets and stars. His beliefs remained the foundation of astronomy for well over a thousand years. This confirmed the accounts in the Bible, so the Church and the scientists were in agreement.

Nicholas Copernicus, born in Poland in 1473, developed a theory that the planets, including the Earth, revolved around the sun. No one paid much attention to this notion, but astronomers did appreciate his mathematical descriptions of the motion of heavenly bodies. These were far more accurate than any which had been produced before.

The great Italian scientist Galileo Galilei, who was born in 1564, twenty years after Copernicus's death, began looking through a telescope he built and described what he saw. His observations convinced him that Copernicus's theory was correct. But when Galileo published his findings, Church leaders forced him to say that he had made a mistake, that he had been wrong in saying that the sun did not revolve around the earth.

Near the end of the 16th Century, Galileo Galilei built a telescope and began viewing the heavens. His observations convinced him that the theory that the Earth and the other planets revolved around the sun was correct. This theory had been developed by Nicholas Copernicus in the previous century, but no one believed him. When Galileo published his findings, the Catholic Church threatened to excommunicate him unless he said that his findings were not true. Because he was a devout Catholic, Galileo obeyed even though he knew he was right.

Astronomers kept building telescopes and looking through them. What they saw provided more and more proof that the Earth and the other planets revolved around the sun, in spite of the Catholic Church's efforts to discourage them.

In Germany early in the seventeenth century, Johannes Kepler published his laws of planetary motion. Later in the century, the Englishman Sir Isaac Newton discovered the law of gravity and demonstrated that the movements of stars and planets could be predicted, which made astronomy much more accurate. German-born William Herschel spent most of his life in England, where he used his homemade telescope to discover the planet Uranus in the eighteenth century and show that the solar system was much bigger than anyone had previously imagined.

At the end of the nineteenth century, a wealthy American named Charles Yerkes donated what was then the world's largest telescope, a 40-inch refractor, to the University of Chicago. He also built the observatory that would house the telescope. What became known as the Yerkes Observatory is located at Lake Geneva in Wisconsin, about 75 miles from the bright lights of Chicago.

Soon afterwards many of the best astronomers working with the Yerkes Telescope were lured to California by a still bigger telescope, the 60-inch reflector at Mount Wilson Observatory near Pasadena. This in turn would be dwarfed by the 100-inch reflecting telescope at Mount Wilson that would be ready just as World War I began in 1917.

The development of large telescopes in the United States occurred just as the young Edwin Hubble began his career as an astronomer. It was these telescopes that would make his observations possible. His observations, in turn, would reveal a universe of a vastness never before imagined.

In just a few centuries, Earth had been shaken from the secure position it had occupied for thousands of years. It was no longer the center of the universe. It was only a relatively small planet among several that orbited the sun. And by the time eight-year-old Edwin Hubble spent the night of his birthday looking through his grandfather's telescope, astronomers had realized that not only was the Earth not the center of the universe, neither was the sun.

The sun was only one of billions of stars in our galaxy, called the Milky Way because the thick band of stars from the galaxy look like a stream of milk that had spilled across the night sky. But at least the astronomers were confident that this enormous galaxy was the entire universe.

They were, that is, until Edwin Hubble grew up.

Basketball

High School was very fortunate, this year, in securing Mr. Hubble, a former basketball star of the University of Chicago, to coach the team.

Mr. Hubble, with the material afforded, was able to build up a team that defeated every team of any consequence in this section of Indiana, and in Kentucky.

The team this year was, without a doubt, the best that New Albany has ever had. Before going to Bloomington it had a perfect record, having defeated the teams from Salem, New Albany Y. M. C. A., Lexington and Henderson (Ky.), and many other teams of note.

In the tournament at Bloomington they started off in fine manner, winning the first two games on the schedule, but the third was lost to the team from Clinton High School. This defeat eliminated them from the race and they were forced to come home without the coveted championship. They made a fine showing, however, and the students are as proud of them as if they had won the State championship.

At the close of the tournament, Fawcett and Joseph were picked on the All-State Second Team, while Daniel was picked among the six best centers.

The students of the school showed their school spirit by collecting a purse of about forty dollars to pay the team's expenses to Bloomington and by giving them a reception when they returned.

30

Edwin Hubble told his wife and other people he wanted to impress that he had been a successful lawyer in Kentucky after he returned from studying in England on a Rhodes Scholarship. In fact he never passed the bar exam and was a high school teacher. Family friend Jack Roberts saved this photo of Hubble from the school yearbook. He really was a schoolteacher in New Albany, Indiana.

Chapter 2

Early Years

Edwin Hubble was born on November 20, 1889 in Marshfield, Missouri to John and Jennie Hubble. The first child in the family had been Edwin's older brother Henry, the second his sister Lucy. Then came Edwin. Five more children would follow: Bill, Virginia (who died soon after her first birthday), Helen, Emma, and Betsy. Much of the information about the Hubble family life during the years when Edwin was growing up comes from his sisters, Helen Hubble Lane and Betsy Hubble. They shared their memories with Hubble's biographer, Gale Christianson.

John Hubble, Edwin's father, was not an easy man to live with. He was stern and distant, a severe disciplinarian who expected his children to follow strict rules and gave them chores to develop their sense of responsibility. Edwin frequently suffered under his father's rigid pronouncements. However, John Hubble was frequently away from home on business trips. The children were raised primarily by their warm and fun-loving mother, Jennie.

Edwin liked to visit his grandparents, and particularly his mother's father, William Henderson James. His grandpa James was fascinated by the stars, and had built a telescope in his back yard. This was the telescope that Edwin stayed up to look through on the night of his eighth birthday. Even after he no longer lived near his grandfather, Edwin wrote him letters about astronomy. When he was twelve years old he wrote a letter discussing the possibility of life on Mars. Mr. James thought it was so interesting that he sent it to the local newspaper to be published.

John Hubble had trained to be a lawyer but instead worked in the insurance business. He changed employers several times, so the family moved frequently. Finally they settled in the Chicago area. John chose Wheaton, a suburb of Chicago, as a place to live because it was a white Protestant community that banned the sale of alcohol.

The Hubble family attended the First Baptist Church in Wheaton. Edwin's father served as a trustee of the church and his mother taught Sunday school. Edwin sang in the choir.

At first, Edwin's performance in school was not so good. The reason seemed to be his attitude more than his ability. He was frequently disrespectful toward his teachers. His classmates reported that he was distant and had few friends. By the time he entered fourth grade, however, his marks began to improve. When the family moved to Wheaton, Edwin was put into the eighth grade even though he hadn't even turned twelve.

Edwin was also a good athlete, enjoying many sports and excelling at them. He reached his full height of six feet, two inches by the time he was a junior in high school. He played basketball and football. His best sport may have been track, where he competed in track meets in the high jump, pole vault, shot put, discus and hammer throw. He even set a state record in the high jump.

He got good grades in high school, but continued to receive low marks for citizenship because he remained aloof and arrogant with his peers and challenged his teachers' authority. During the ceremonies at Edwin's high school graduation, the superintendent of schools announced sternly, "Edwin Hubble, I have watched you for four years and I have never seen you study for ten minutes." Then he smiled and went on, "Here is a scholarship to the University of Chicago."

Edwin Hubble was still sixteen years old when he entered the University of Chicago in 1906. He already had decided that he wanted one of the newly created Rhodes Scholarships when he graduated. These very competitive scholarships, which are still awarded every year, include all living expenses and some spending money while the student studies at one of England's finest universities, either Cambridge or Oxford.

Many of his choices in college were made with this goal in mind. He had another goal in mind: he wanted to be an astronomer. But he knew that his father wouldn't agree to "anything so outlandish," which was Betsy Hubble's memory of their father's attitude toward Edwin's choice of career. John Hubble wanted his son to become a lawyer.

Edwin satisfied his father by taking the courses that were required for entrance to law school. He satisfied himself by taking the math and science courses that he knew he would need for advanced study in astronomy.

There was another conflict with his father. Edwin wanted to play college football, and the coach very much wanted him to. John Hubble, however, had forbidden Edwin to play football on the grounds that it was a dangerous sport. Edwin's efforts to change his father's mind not only failed, they backfired. In an effort to convince his father to let him play football, he made a list of all the injuries that had occurred in one of John Hubble's favorite sports, baseball.

The only result was that John Hubble also forbade his son to play baseball.

Oddly enough his father did not object to boxing, so although it was not a university sport, Edwin Hubble boxed at the local YMCA with some success (although probably not as much success as he later claimed). He continued to participate in basketball and track during his college years as he had in high school. This was partially because he loved sports, but it was also because being an athlete was one of the requirements for a Rhodes Scholarship.

Another requirement was demonstrating leadership potential. Edwin ran unopposed for vice president of his senior class just a month before the selection of the scholarship winner. He also sang and performed in musical comedies.

All of his determination and efforts were successful. Edwin was voted the Rhodes Scholar from Illinois in 1910. Even though he was finally on his own and no longer dependent on his family, Edwin chose to attend Queen's College at Oxford to study law as his father wanted him to, rather than taking advanced courses in science and mathematics at Cambridge. But he also found time to study astronomy.

Edwin was so enchanted by all things English that he made every effort to become more British than the British themselves—the upper-class British of course. At Queen's College his classmates were members of the nobility and future statesmen.

Edwin began wearing English clothes such as capes and knickers—baggy knee-length pants—and carrying a cane. He also began speaking with an English accent and

Hubble, second from left, rear, had recently returned from his Rhodes Scholarship year in England when this photo was taken. He is with a group of hikers enjoying the countryside just west of New Albany, Indiana where he taught school.

using the more formal and aloof manners of the British upper class. These habits he continued throughout his life, a practice that many people considered to be snobbish and phony.

He made friends with many of his English classmates, and was frequently invited to spend weekends on their country estates. He traveled to other European countries, particularly Germany, during school holidays. He also spent time with Herbert Hall Turner, Professor of Astronomy at Oxford, both at the Turners' home and at the university observatory where Turner was the director.

In January, 1913, his father died after being in ill health for several years. It was nearing the end of Edwin's three years at Oxford. He wrote to his mother pledging his help when he returned from England at the end of the school term. He said he would practice law and promised her that the family would all live together after his return.

But things would work out far differently from what he told his mother.

While Edwin Hubble was teaching school in New Albany, Indiana, he brought a telescope to entertain his students. He set it up in the driveway of his friend John Roberts, who took this photo late in the day. It is the earliest photograph showing Hubble with a telescope.

Chapter 3

The Star-Gazer Returns

The stories about Edwin Hubble's life during the year after he returned from England differ depending on who is telling the story. According to his own account he had a very successful law practice in Kentucky, where the family had moved in 1910. According to his sisters' recollections, he was a schoolteacher in nearby New Albany, Indiana. The official records show that he never passed the Kentucky bar exams, and several students from New Albany remembered this oddly dressed teacher of Spanish, physics, and mathematics who spoke with an English accent.

Edwin's intention to help the family financially didn't work out very well. Not only did he not help, he also invested what little money his mother had in a business venture that failed. His sister Betsy recalled that he expected his mother to prepare English teas for his Rhodes Scholar friends every Sunday because he was homesick for England.

Whatever the details of that year may have been—and it seems that Hubble's stories about his own life were largely romantic fictions—Edwin's promise to his mother to keep the family together lasted only a year. He wrote to his former astronomy professor at the University of Chicago to ask for help.

The professor wrote to the director of the university's Yerkes Observatory in Wisconsin, suggesting that Hubble be given an assistantship that would include a tuition scholarship plus room and board.

There were two things that Edwin Hubble was very good at. One was observing the stars. The other was impressing the people whom he wanted to impress. Both of these abilities served him well with Dr. Edwin Frost, the Director of Yerkes Observatory. Frost suggested that Hubble should arrive for the annual meeting of the Astronomical Society of America on the campus of Northwestern University. The director also submitted Hubble's name for membership in the organization.

At this conference, astronomer Vesto Slipher read a paper giving evidence that most nebulae (mysterious cloudy shapes) were speeding away from the Solar System at amazing velocities. This indicated that our galaxy, the Milky Way, might not be the entire universe as had been thought until then. Slipher's theory about the nebulae indicated that there might be other galaxies containing millions and millions of stars just as the Milky Way did.

Edwin Hubble began his work at Yerkes Observatory in October of 1914. Perhaps inspired by Slipher's paper on the motion of nebulae, Hubble began long hours of patiently observing and photographing nebulae. Each exposure lasted for more than two hours, and by the time he left Edwin would have more than a thousand.

While Edwin was at the Yerkes Observatory, his mother and sisters and brother Henry rented a small house in Madison, Wisconsin in hopes of keeping the family together. Another brother, Bill, was in the army and sent his paychecks to support his mother and sisters. Even though Edwin was only 60 miles away, his work was so engrossing that they saw little of him. Then he moved back to Chicago to work on his Ph.D. degree.

Meanwhile, in California a new 100-inch reflecting telescope was nearly ready at Mount Wilson Observatory. The director was George Ellery Hale, who had been at Yerkes before moving west. Hale offered Hubble a position.

In April 1917, before Hubble could move to California to begin working at Mount Wilson, the United States declared war on Germany. Edwin wrote to Hale telling him that he intended to apply for a commission as an officer and fight for his country. "His country" in this case applied to his beloved England as much as to the United States. He would be serving in the U.S. Army, but it was England that he would be defending from the German attacks. He asked Hale to hold the position for him until the war was over. Hale agreed.

Edwin Hubble was soon to be Captain Hubble, a battalion commander in the 86th (Black Hawks) Division. In December of 1917 he was promoted to major. He liked the military life with its order, discipline, and efficiency, and he liked his high rank and the respect that went with it. By the time Major Hubble's unit finally arrived in Europe, the war was nearly over. Although he later said that he was wounded in action, the records show that his division arrived too late to see any combat.

In August of 1919 Edwin Hubble returned to the United States and went immediately to Pasadena, California, the location of the observatory headquarters. At that time Pasadena was still a small town of about 20,000 people. The telescope itself was about 60 miles away, high in the San Gabriel Mountains. Little work had been done during the war years.

Edwin Hubble would soon make up for lost time.

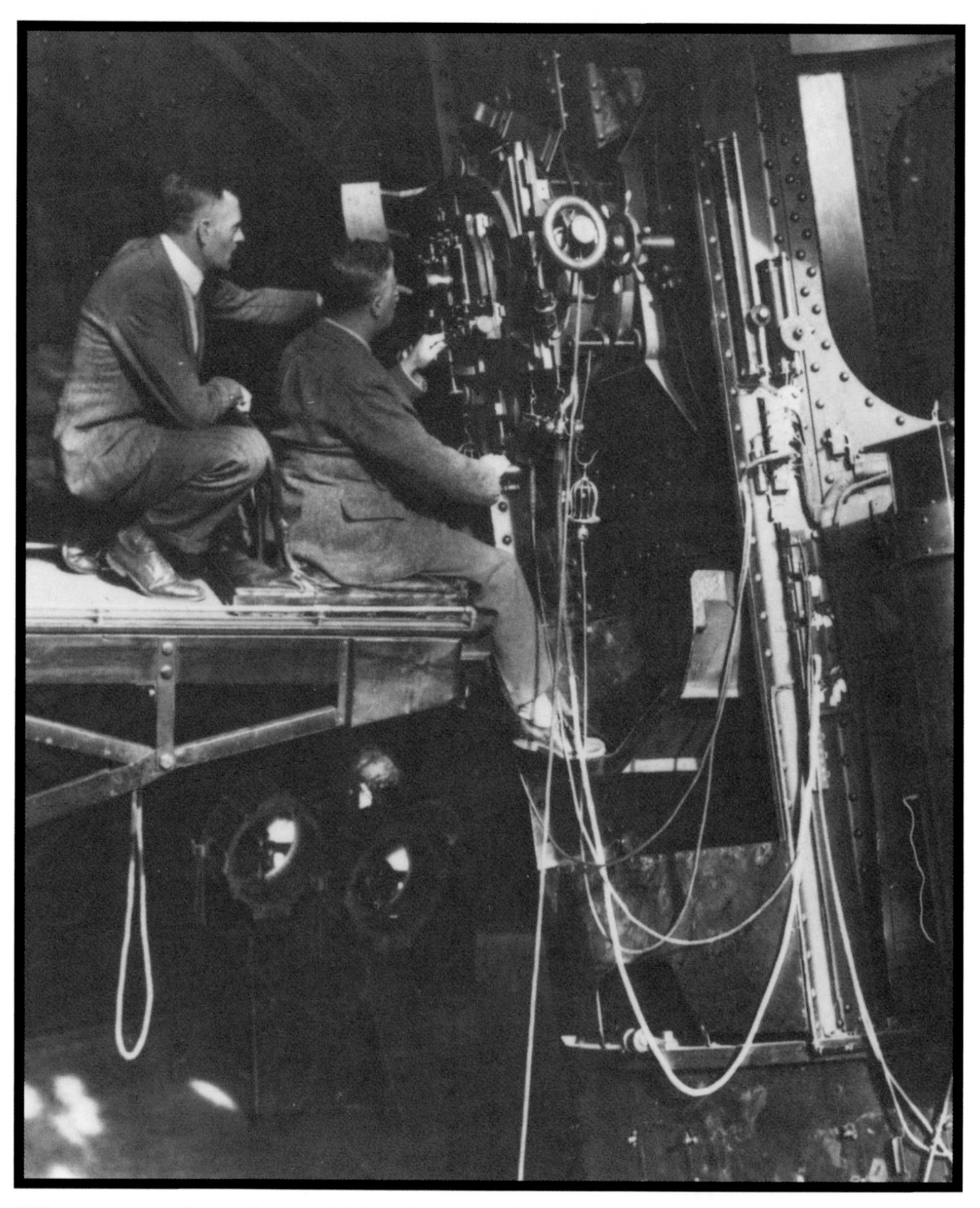

When completed in 1917, the Hooker 100-inch telescope at Mount Wilson Observatory near Pasadena, California (shown here) became the largest telescope in the world at that time. This picture shows astronomers Edwin Hubble and Sir James Hopwood Jeans using the telescope. It was with this telescope that Hubble's universe-shaking photographs of a Cepheid star in the Andromeda Galaxy were taken.

Chapter 4

Three Midwesterners

When Hubble arrived at Mount Wilson, he was in uniform even though he had left the army. Like the British, he retained his military title into civilian life, and was known ever after as "The Major" by the staff at the observatory. He added his army boots and field jacket to his wardrobe of British style-shirts and knickers, and continued to speak with an English accent.

At least one of his fellow astronomers thought he was ridiculous and made no secret of his opinion. This man was Harlow Shapley. He was also from Missouri, and had been at Mount Wilson for five years by the time Hubble arrived. Shapley sometimes said that he was an "accidental astronomer." He had left school after the fifth grade and later became a crime reporter on small-town newspapers. He soon repented of his lack of education and went back to school, graduating from high school at the age of 21. He planned to major in journalism at the University of Missouri. When the opening of the journalism school was postponed for a year, he opened the college catalogue and signed up for the first course he could pronounce. He skipped "archaeology" and enrolled in "astronomy."

Shapley did so well in his accidental field of study that he didn't transfer to the journalism school after it opened. He ended up being the university's only astronomy major, continued another year for an M.A. degree, and then was awarded a fellowship at the Princeton University Observatory. He was a hard worker. His specialty was the

Milky Way Galaxy, which he believed to be the entire universe but considerably larger than it was previously thought to be.

Unlike Hubble, Shapley was proud of his Missouri background. He never adopted the cultivated manner of speech of educated people even though he had graduated from Princeton with highest honors and had published nearly a hundred scientific papers by 1920. He had no use for people that he called "high hats," and he thought Edwin Hubble was one of them.

There was another midwesterner on the mountain besides the two antagonistic Missourians. Milton Humason was born in Minnesota but his family soon moved to California. Called "Milt" by everyone who knew him, Humason was an even more unlikely astronomer than Harlow Shapley. Shapley left school but later went back. Humason left school at the age of fourteen with no intention of going back. He went to summer camp on Mount Wilson, and fell in love with the area.

While he was still in his teens, Milt got a job as a mule driver bringing lumber up the mountain for the observatory's facilities. He married the daughter of the chief engineer at Mount Wilson, and when he learned that there was a position open for a janitor he applied for it. He was hired as relief night assistant for the 60-inch telescope, then for the 100-inch when it was ready.

A visiting astronomy student taught Humason how to use the astrographic camera to photograph stars. He was so good at it that he carried on alone after the student left. Harlow Shapley noticed Humason's skill and began having him take plates for his projects. The two midwestern small town boys also enjoyed playing poker and having a drink or two on cloudy nights.

Unlike Harlow Shapley, the more accepting Milt Humason did not find Edwin Hubble's English mannerisms and aloof manner offensive. Years later Humason recorded his first impression of Hubble.

"My own first meeting with Hubble occurred when he was just beginning observations on Mount Wilson," Humason said in an account published in Gale Christianson's *Edwin Hubble: Mariner of the Nebulae.* "I received a vivid impression of the man that night that has remained with me over the years. He was photographing at the Newtonian focus of the 60-inch, standing while he did his guiding. His tall, vigorous figure, pipe in mouth, was clearly outlined against the sky. A brisk wind whipped his military trench coat around his body and occasionally blew sparks from his pipe into the darkness of the dome. 'Seeing' that night was rated extremely poor on our Mount Wilson scale, but when Hubble came back from developing his plate in the dark room he was jubilant. 'If this is an example of poor seeing conditions,' he said, 'I shall always be able to get usable photographs with the Mount Wilson instruments.' The confidence and enthusiasm, which he showed on that night, were typical of the way he approached all his problems. He was sure of himself—of what he wanted to do, and of how to do it."

Hubble and Humason had very different educational backgrounds, very different attitudes and lifestyles. But they shared what was for both of them the central core and most important part of their lives: the long dark hours spent observing and photographing the night skies. They were both outstanding observers, both perfectionists in their handling of the telescopes and their technique in the darkroom developing photographic plates. Over the years they developed—in addition to thousands of photographs of the stars—a deep respect for each other.

From the very beginning of his work at Mount Wilson, Hubble concentrated his efforts on observing and photographing nebulae and classifying them. The word "nebula" comes from the Latin word for "cloud." Nebulae were cloudy patches astronomers had observed but didn't know what they were. It was believed that there were different types of nebulae. Several astronomers had presented systems of classification, but none of these systems were generally agreed on.

Harlow Shapley was convinced that however many types of nebulae there might be, all of them were within the Milky Way Galaxy. Edwin Hubble did not agree.

Milt Humason was content to take his beautifully precise photographs and measurements and let others interpret the findings.

During his first years at Mount Wilson, Hubble was able to demonstrate that nebulae within the Milky Way Galaxy were the result of the light from stars being diffused by cosmic dust. These nebulae, he wrote, "re-emit at each point exactly the amount of light radiations which they receive from the stars." If there were no stars nearby, "the clouds of material present themselves as dark nebulosity."

This problem solved, Hubble turned his attention to nebulae that he thought might not be contained within the Milky Way. He analyzed hundreds of photographs taken by himself, by Humason and Shapley, and by other astronomers, and came up with four types of extragalactic nebulae. At first no one paid any attention to his work. It took many years before Hubble's classification was seriously considered, but it is the classification that is used today.

No one has found a more accurate system than Hubble devised before he even proved that these nebulae were outside of our galaxy and indeed are galaxies themselves. He found that the types were spiral, elongated, globular, and irregular. The last category included any nebula that couldn't be placed in one of the other three groups. He felt there was no need for further types because irregular nebulae occurred so seldom.

Hale, the director of Mount Wilson Observatory, thought that Hubble should publish his system of classification immediately. In marked contrast to his tendency to exaggerate his achievements in other areas, however, Hubble was always extremely cautious about his theories in astronomy. In this instance he preferred to submit his classification to the International Astronomical Union's commission on nebulae. Unfortunately the chairman of the committee had a classification of his own that he insisted on using. Hubble's classification was ignored. Not until several years later did Hubble send a paper on extragalactic nebulae to the *Astrophysical Journal.* The article not only gave descriptions but showed photographs of all of the types.

In the meantime, Harlow Shapley had accepted a position as head of the astronomy department at Harvard University. The two Missourians (both as stubborn as natives of the "Show-Me" state have the reputation for being) could now pursue their separate theories on different sides of the continent.

Shown in this optical telescopic image are Galaxy M31 (Andromeda Galaxy) and Galaxy M33 (Triangulum Galaxy) which is almost a satellite of M31. Hubble's observations of cepheid variable stars in these galaxies was the first proof that galaxies other than the Milky Way existed. His work with Cepheids enabled him to tell how far away their galaxies were and demonstrate that they could not be within the Milky Way.

Chapter 5

The Perfect Couple

In June of 1920 a young woman visited the Mount Wilson Observatory at the urging of a couple who were her friends. If Milt Humason's first view of Edwin Hubble had been somewhat romantic, it was nothing to the image Grace Burke Lieb recorded after seeing Hubble studying a photographic plate.

"This should not have seemed unusual, an astronomer examining a plate against the light," she wrote in her diary. "But if the astronomer looked an Olympian, tall, strong, and beautiful, with the shoulders of the Hermes of Praxiteles (a famous Greek statue), and the benign serenity, it became unusual. There was a sense of power, channeled and directed in an adventure that had nothing to do with personal ambition and its anxieties and lack of peace. There was hard concentrated effort and yet detachment. The power was controlled."

Grace was married at the time. In fact the woman visiting the observatory with her was her husband's sister. But a year later Grace's husband, a geologist, was killed in a mining accident. She returned to the home of her wealthy and socially prominent parents. Edwin Hubble began courting her.

The romantic Grace was the perfect audience for Hubble's tales. He told her about his heroic exploits in battle, his successful law career, his adventures fighting brigands in the north woods, his rescues of ladies from drowning, his defeat of champions in the boxing ring—and many other deeds that never happened. At least the only record of them is in Grace's diary where she faithfully recorded everything her hero told her.

Grace's wealthy parents were also impressed with Hubble's stories. Of course that meant that he had to be sure they never met any members of his family, and they never did. Grace and Edwin were married on February 26, 1924 and were almost never apart until his death nearly 30 years later. His sisters reported that they never met Edwin's wife, nor did anyone else in the Hubble family.

During the period when Hubble was courting Grace, he was also involved in making one of the most important discoveries in the history of astronomy. The debate over whether the Milky Way Galaxy was the entire universe, or whether there were other similar galaxies outside the boundaries of the Milky Way, had been going on for years.

In 1920 the National Academy of Sciences had organized a debate between two leading astronomers, Herbert Curtis and Harlow Shapley. Curtis believed that spiral nebulae were "individual galaxies, or island universes, comparable with our own galaxy." Shapley contended, "The spirals are not composed of typical stars at all, but are truly nebulous objects." These objects, he said, were within our galaxy.

But the debate went nowhere because it took place entirely as one theory against another. Neither side was able to provide any proof. Edwin Hubble agreed with Curtis that the spiral nebulae were "island universes," galaxies like our own at enormous distances from us. And Edwin Hubble was able to prove it.

Astronomers had been observing the Andromeda nebula ever since the nineteenth century. When the 100-

inch telescope at Mount Wilson began operating, observations intensified. Several novae, stars that suddenly increase in brightness due to explosions of gases, had been detected in the Andromeda nebula. In the summer of 1923, Hubble began using both the 60-inch and 100-inch telescopes to gather information about these novae. In October he realized that one of the stars that had been labeled as a nova was not a nova at all. It was a variable star. On the photographic plate he crossed out the "N" for nova and wrote in large letters, "VAR!" to indicate that the star was a variable.

To understand the importance of this discovery, it is necessary to know something about the Cepheids, which is what these variable stars are called. The amount of brightness that a Cepheid gives off is not constant. The brightness varies, or changes, according to a definite cycle. These cycles vary in length from several hours to more than a month.

Henrietta Leavitt, a researcher at the Harvard Observatory, had catalogued hundreds of variable stars during the early years of the twentieth century. In 1908 she published data that showed that the cycle of a Cepheid star corresponded to its brightness. The longer it took for a star to go through its entire cycle from dim to bright to dim again, the brighter the star was (this is called its magnitude). If two Cepheids had the same cycle, they would also have the same magnitude. Therefore, if astronomers found a Cepheid star, they could measure its distance by comparing its apparent brightness with its known brightness.

Ironically, the astronomer who had done the most work with Cepheids, both at Mount Wilson and at Harvard, was

Harlow Shapley. By working with known Cepheids within the Milky Way, Shapley had demonstrated that the size of our galaxy was far larger than had been previously believed. Before Shapley's work the galaxy was thought to be no more than 30,000 light years in diameter. Shapley found that the planet Earth is part of a solar system close to the edge of the Milky Way rather than in the center as had formerly been thought. He also found that our galaxy is 300,000 light years in diameter, ten times the previous estimate. This "Big Galaxy," as Shapley called it, was the universe, in his opinion.

With increasing excitement but with his usual cautious and precise methods of making observations, Hubble concentrated on the variable star he had found in the Andromeda nebula. He went back through the photographic plates that had been taken by other astronomers at Mount Wilson. He measured the period of the variable and plotted its brightness curve. In early February of 1924 there was perfect viewing weather for a week and he was able to observe the star's brightness increasing rapidly.

No astronomer before Hubble had ever tried to find Cepheids in the Andromeda nebula. Now that he had found one, he had only to compare its known brightness with its apparent brightness and he would have the distance to the nebula. His measurements indicated that the Cepheid was about a million light years away. That meant that it was far beyond the furthest boundaries of the Milky Way. To astronomers, this conclusion was staggering. The Milky Way was not the only galaxy in the universe. Soon it would become evident that there were millions of other galaxies.

Hubble's first announcement of his findings was a letter to Harlow Shapley at Harvard. The letter was written in technical terms and included a graph showing the light curve of the Cepheid's cycle.

A young graduate student was in Shapley's office when he received Hubble's letter. She later reported that Shapley handed her the letter and said, "Here is the letter that has destroyed my universe." Shapley had immediately understood the meaning of Hubble's observations, but he wasn't about to give "high hat" Hubble the satisfaction of admitting it. Shapley wrote back saying that Hubble's letter about variable stars in the Andromeda nebula "is the most entertaining piece of literature I have seen for a long time."

Hubble may have made up stories about other areas of his life, but never about anything as important as his astronomical observations. He was if anything over-cautious in reporting his findings. It was many months before the significance of the discovery of the Cepheid in the Andromeda nebula was revealed to the world.

In the middle of March the newly married Hubbles set sail for Europe and an extended honeymoon. Edwin took Grace to Oxford and Cambridge and other favorite places from his Rhodes Scholar days. The Hubbles were guests of honor at a dinner of the Royal Astronomical Society where Hubble spoke about his classification system for nebulae.

Edwin and Grace also traveled in France, Switzerland, and Italy. Everywhere they went they were in the company of the European aristocracy they so admired and imitated. They returned to California late in May.

In January 1931, the men who revolutionized our concept of the universe met in the Observatories library of the Carnegie Institution of Washington. Shown left to right: Milton L. Humason, Edwin Hubble, Charles E. St. John, Albert A. Michelson, Albert Einstein, William W. Campbell, Walter S. Adams. A portrait of George Ellery Hale, one of the founders of modern astrophysics, is in the background.

Chapter 6

Hubble's Law

On November 23, 1924, an article in the *New York Times* revealed Hubble's discovery to the public: "Confirmation of the view that spiral nebulae, which appear in the heavens as whirling clouds, are in reality distant stellar systems or 'island universes,' has been obtained by Dr. Edwin Hubbell."

Except for misspelling his name, the article about Hubble's work was accurate and clear. Although American astronomers had by then heard about this breakthrough, Hubble hadn't published anything. The public read about it before the scientific community did.

The next problem Edwin Hubble set out to solve was finding out the speed at which galaxies were traveling through space. Hubble and Milt Humason worked closely together. Their work was based on the spectrograph, which analyzes stars by passing their light through a gas that breaks the light into a spectrum, or pattern of colored lines. A spectrum resembles a rainbow with red at one end and violet on the other. This enables scientists to find the chemical makeup of the stars.

Vesto Slipher had found that stars and nebulae moving away from the observer had their spectra shifted toward the red end of the spectrum, and stars and nebulae moving toward the observer had spectra shifted toward the violet end. This occurs because light waves act like sound waves. Their apparent frequency changes by compressing when approaching and stretching out when going away. This is why the sound of a siren seems to change as it passes you.

By determining the distance to galaxies containing Cepheid stars and then using a spectrum analysis to determine the galaxy's velocity, Hubble was able to show that there is a direct relationship between the distance of a galaxy from the Earth and the speed at which it is traveling. If the distance doubles, the speed doubles. The further away a galaxy is, the greater the velocity at which it is hurtling away from the Earth. This relationship between speed and distance came to be called Hubble's Law, or the law of redshifts.

Hubble and Humason took hundreds of spectra of galaxies so distant that no individual stars or clusters could be observed. Using his formula showing the relationship between speed and distance, Hubble was able to tell how far away a galaxy was by determining how fast it was traveling. The results were astonishing. They showed that the universe is expanding, exploding actually, with all of the galaxies hurtling away from each other at enormous speeds—and the further they are from each other, the greater the speeds.

The tremendous velocities at which galaxies are traveling away from each other are the foundation of what is called the "Big Bang" theory. The theory suggests that at some time billions of years ago the universe was created by an explosion and has been expanding ever since.

In January of 1929 both Humason and Hubble submitted short papers to the National Academy of Science. Humason's paper reported on measuring the velocity of a galaxy. Hubble's was titled "A Relation Between Distance and Radial Velocity Among Extra-Galactic Nebulae." This paper is now regarded as one of the most important developments in the history of astronomy.

In spite of the importance of Hubble's discoveries and the fame that came with them, he had difficulties at the Mount Wilson Observatory. Director Walter Adams, who had replaced Hale, was upset by Hubble's frequent absences and by his insistence that he should be paid while he and Grace were traveling.

Edwin and Grace Hubble enjoyed their position in high society both in America and in Europe. On their frequent trips to England they visited the rich and famous. Members of the nobility, noted intellectuals and artists, and fellow scientists entertained the couple lavishly. Hubble said this international acclaim and the lectures he gave were positive public relations for the observatory. Therefore he should receive his salary while he and Grace were enjoying the hospitality of friends abroad.

Their active social life continued when they were at home in Pasadena. Hubble continued to be very distant and aloof, even haughty, with other staff members at Mount Wilson (with the exception of Humason). But the celebrities Edwin and Grace cultivated saw another side of him. His interest in stars was not limited to the ones he looked at through the telescopes. Some of the most famous and celebrated personalities of the day were friends of the Hubbles. Edwin was known for his hospitality and his storytelling, Grace for being a gracious hostess.

When the famous English writer Aldous Huxley came to Hollywood to work on screenplays, he and his wife became close friends of the Hubbles. So did actor Charlie Chaplin, animator and filmmaker Walt Disney, and author Anita Loos. Film director Frank Capra invited the Hubbles to the Academy Award ceremonies where Capra introduced Hubble as "the world's greatest living astronomer." The world's most famous scientist, Albert Einstein, and his wife Elsa also visited the Hubbles. Hubble's work demonstrating that the universe was expanding had changed Einstein's opinion that the universe was stable.

While the rest of the United States struggled through poverty and joblessness in the Great Depression of the 1930's, the Hubbles lived a seemingly enchanted life at expensive hotels and restaurants and resorts. Often Edwin would give his famous friends tours of the observatory.

By the end of the 1930's, Hubble and Humason had taken their observations to the limit of the viewing possibilities of the 100-inch telescope. They were anxiously awaiting the completion of a new 200-inch telescope on Mount Palomar, about 40 miles northeast of San Diego. Once more, however, the completion of a telescope had to be postponed for a war. Once again Germany was attacking other European countries. Once again Edwin Hubble urged the United States to enter the war on the side of England.

During World War II, Edwin Hubble again wanted to serve his country, although he was now in his 50's and too old for the Army. He served at the Aberdeen Proving Ground on Chesapeake Bay from 1942 until the end of the war. As head of ballistics he supervised the testing of bombs and shells. The only housing the Hubbles could find was a small house, little more than a shack, near the firing range. They preferred that to being separated.

When Hubble returned to Pasadena and to the Mount Wilson Observatory after the war, a major disappointment awaited him. Walter Adams, the director of the observatory, was retiring, and Hubble wanted to be the next director. Adams, who had been battling with Hubble for years over his frequent absences, did everything he could to prevent Hubble's appointment. In addition to his other problems with him, Adams pointed out that Hubble frequently failed to answer letters, did not appear at committee meetings, and in general had shown no liking for administrative work. The position was given to Ira Bowen, an astrophysicist from Caltech.

Between Hubble's disappointment at not being named director of the observatory and the frustration of waiting for the 200-inch Hale Telescope at Mt. Palomar to be ready, it was a difficult time. The giant instrument was finally dedicated in June of 1948, and Edwin Hubble had the honor of processing the first plates to be taken with it. There were still problems, however, and the images were not as clear as they should have been. Palomar was closed again.

Grace and Edwin departed for England and the social whirl that never failed to cheer him up. He was elected Honorary Fellow of Oxford University's Queen's College, the first Rhodes Scholar to be honored with that title. When reporters asked Hubble how he had felt when he looked through the huge telescope at Palomar, he said, "I thought I was blasé, but I got all excited about it."

The following year, in July of 1949, Grace and Edwin were vacationing at one of their favorite resorts in Colorado when the 59-year-old astronomer suffered a severe heart attack. His wife tried to keep the news of his serious illness from the public, and even the staff at Mount Wilson didn't realize how ill Hubble was. He was unable to get to his office until October. His colleagues were shocked to see how he had aged. His doctors would not allow him to work at the high altitudes of Mount Palomar.

At this time Allan Sandage, a young astronomer who would become one of the most respected in the field during the latter half of the 20th Century, was appointed to act as Hubble's observing assistant. Sandage later said that he didn't know which was more frightening, Hubble or the universe. But in spite of the awe he felt, Sandage did an excellent job. With his help, and the continuing excellent observations and photography of Milt Humason, Hubble was able to continue measuring the velocities of ever-more-distant galaxies.

In 1953, the Hubbles took one last trip to Europe. He gave a lecture before the Royal Astronomical Society and was invited by the young Queen Elizabeth II to speak at a formal event. Grace and Edwin traveled to Scotland where Hubble went fly fishing, one of his favorite activities.

When they returned to California, Hubble's doctors felt he was well enough to go up the mountain. He made a trip to Palomar on September 1, excited to be back at the big telescope. Back at his office in Pasadena, he kept busy with classifying previously taken photographic plates. On September 28, Grace was driving him home for lunch when he had a final heart attack.

He was dead by the time the doctor arrived.

In a paper written for the Royal Astronomical Society of Canada in 1989 for the centennial celebration of Edwin

Hubble's birth, Allan Sandage reflected on Hubble's career. According to Sandage, between 1922 and 1936 Hubble "solved four of the central problems in cosmology, any one of which would have guaranteed him a position of the first rank in history."

Sandage identified these four central problems:

1. Between 1922 and 1926 Hubble proposed a classification for nebulae, both galactic and extragalactic, which has become standard.

2. His discovery of Cepheids in the Andromeda nebula settled the question of the nature of galaxies, that they were "island universes" like our own Milky Way.

3. From 1926 to 1936 he determined that the distribution of galaxies is homogeneous in distance.

4. The velocity-distance relation, or Hubble's Law, was demonstrated in a series of papers written with Milton Humason between 1931 and 1936 and formed the basis of the "Big Bang" theory of an expanding universe.

Despite Sandage's praise, however, Edwin Hubble did not receive all of the honors that he believed he deserved during his lifetime. Probably the major reason was that it was difficult to be sure, during the time that important discoveries were being made, which ones would stand the test of time and which would turn out to need later revision. Another reason was that Hubble's arrogance offended many of his fellow astronomers. When he did not agree with their findings he was not very diplomatic. And his snobbishness irritated many people.

He was never awarded the Nobel Prize, something that he and his wife had hoped for. Quite likely he would have been nominated the year that he died, but the Nobel is not given after death.

Several decades after his death he received an especially meaningful memorial. On April 14, 1990, the space shuttle *Discovery* carried a telescope into orbit around the Earth. The new telescope was about the size of a school bus and weighed twelve tons. Astronomers were excited. At last a telescope was free of the distortions produced by the earth's atmosphere. No longer would their observations depend on good weather.

The telescope was named for Edwin Hubble.

But the first images beamed back to earth were out of focus and fuzzy. For a while, there was even talk that the telescope was worthless.

Three and a half years later, the shuttle *Endeavor* headed into orbit. During a series of dangerous space walks, astronauts fixed the existing problems and added several new instruments.

Just after midnight on December 18, 1993, astronomers waited anxiously for the first photos from the newly repaired Hubble Space Telescope to be beamed to earth.

They were astonished at what they saw.

"It was like being in Washington, D.C., and seeing the light from a firefly in Tokyo, Japan—halfway around the world," wrote Elaine Scott in *Close Encounters: Exploring the Universe with the Hubble Space Telescope.* "The Hubble has looked within our solar system and beyond it. It has watched as stars are born and die, as a comet collided with Jupiter, and as matter spews around the edges of black holes."

Sandage pointed out that the precise verification of Hubble's work "can be determined to the satisfaction of the skeptics only by the future use of the Hubble Space Telescope. For this one suspects that Hubble might have been pleased."

Allan Sandage, shown here in 2000, has been involved in the study of astronomical origins and evolution his entire professional life. His work has transformed our understanding of the universe. Much of Sandage's work has augmented Hubble's work on galaxy classification. Sandage has received numerous awards, including the Peter Gruber Cosmology Prize, the Tomalla Prize from the Swiss Physical Society, and the Eddington Medal from the Royal Astronomical Society.

Edwin Powell Hubble Chronology

1889 Born on November 20 in Marshfield, Missouri
1897 Asks to stay up all night to observe stars through his grandfather's microscope as a gift for his eighth birthday
1901 Moves with family to Wheaton, Illinois
1906 Enters the University of Chicago
1910 Awarded Rhodes scholarship to study at Oxford University in England
1913 Father dies; returns home and teaches school for a year
1914 Enters graduate school in astronomy at University of Chicago; elected member of American Astronomical Society; joins staff at Yerkes Observatory
1917 Receives Ph.D. in astronomy from University of Chicago; joins U.S. Army and is made commander of a battalion that goes overseas the following year
1919 Returns to U.S. and joins staff of the Mount Wilson Observatory
1923 Proves that universe contains many galaxies
1924 Marries Grace Burke
1924 Develops a classification for galaxies
1929 Discovers Hubble's Law, which demonstrates that universe is expanding
1936 Publishes book, *The Realm of the Nebulae*
1942 Heads ballistics research program at Aberdeen Proving Ground in Maryland
1945 Returns to Mount Wilson Observatory
1949 Begins work at Mount Palomar, California; has serious heart attack
1953 Dies of heart attack in Pasadena on September 28

Astronomy Time Line

2446 BC Chinese astronomers observe that Mercury, Venus, Earth, Mars and Jupiter are aligned with each other, which shows they knew that the planets move through space.
1600 BC Babylonian astronomers compile star catalogs.
450 BC Greek philosopher Anaxagoras suggests that the sun is a hot rock rather than a god, an idea so ridiculous that he is thrown out of Athens.
145 AD Greek scientist Ptolemy publishes *Almagest*, a thirteen-volume treatise that develops the earth-centered theory of the universe which astronomers use for 1,400 years.

1030 Arab astronomer Al-Sufi of Baghdad creates the best star catalog of the many that appear at about this time.

1543 Polish astronomer Nicolaus Copernicus publishes his book *On the Revolution of the Heavenly Spheres* which proposes that idea that the earth revolves around the sun.

1609 German astronomer Johannes Kepler describes orbits of the planets.

1609 Italian astronomer Galileo Galilei builds a telescope, which he uses to observe the planets and prove Copernicus's theory. He is later forced by the Church to deny this finding.

1668 English astronomer Isaac Newton builds the first reflector telescope.

1687 Isaac Newton publishes his book *Principia*, which proves that Earth and other planets revolve around the sun.

1781 English astronomer William Herschel discovers Uranus.

1846 German astronomers Johann Galle and Heinrich Louis D'Arrest discover the planet Neptune.

1877 Italian astronomer Giovanni Schiaparelli observes what he calls "canali" (channels or grooves) on the planet Mars.

1897 The 40-inch Yerkes Telescope is dedicated.

1908 The 60-inch Hooker Telescope is built at Mount Wilson Observatory.

1912 American astronomer Henrietta Leavitt discovers Cepheid variable stars.

1917 The 100-inch Hooker Telescope is assembled at Mount Wilson Observatory.

1920 American astronomer Vesto Slipher discovers that nebulae are receding.

1923 Edwin Hubble demonstrates that receding nebulae are outside of our galaxy and are in fact themselves galaxies.

1927 Belgian astronomer Georges LeMaitre introduces Big Bang theory, the idea that the universe was formed in a huge explosion.

1930 American astronomer Clyde Tombaugh discovers Pluto.

1948 The 200-inch Hale Telescope is dedicated at Mount Palomar.

1957 The Soviet Union launches Sputnik, the first artificial earth satellite.

1967 English astronomers Antony Hewish and Jocelyn Bell discover pulsars (pulsating radio sources).

1969 U.S. astronaut Neil Armstrong becomes the first man to set foot on the moon.

1977 U.S. astronomers at Cornell University report that planet Uranus is surrounded by rings similar to those on Saturn.

1990 The Hubble Space Telescope is launched.

1993 U.S. astronauts make repairs to Hubble Space Telescope.

2003 Space shuttle Columbia disintegrates on re-entering earth's atmosphere.

Further Reading

For Young Adults

Camp, Carole Ann. *American Astronomers, Searchers and Wonderers.* Springfield, NJ: Enslow Publishers, 1996.

Datnow, Claire. *Edwin Hubble: Discoverer of Galaxies.* Springfield, NJ: Enslow Publishers, 1997.

Fox, Mary Virginia. *Edwin Hubble, American Astronomer.* Danbury, CT: Franklin Watts, 1997.

Macdonald, Fiona. *Edwin Hubble.* Chicago: Heinemann Library, 2001.

Miles, Lisa and Alastair Smith. *Complete Book of Astronomy & Space.* London: Usborne Publishing, Ltd., 1998.

Scott, Elaine. *Close Encounters: Exploring the Universe with the Hubble Space Telescope.* New York: Hyperion Books for Children, 1998.

Works Consulted

Christianson, Gale E. *Edwin Hubble: Mariner of the Nebulae.* New York: Farrar, Straus and Giroux, 1995.

Gribbin, John and Simon Goodwin. *Origins: Our Place in Hubble's Universe.* New York: The Overlook Press, 1998.

Hubble, Edwin Powell. Original papers and correspondence, The Huntington Library, California Institute of Technology, San Marino, California.

Hubble, Edwin Powell. Original photographs. Archives, Carnegie Institution, Mt. Wilson Observatory, 1919-1953.

Sharov, Alexander S. and Igor D. Novikov. *Edwin Hubble, the Discoverer of the Big Bang Universe.* Great Britain: Cambridge University Press, 1993.

On the Internet

Sandage Lecture on Hubble—www.antwrp.gsfc.nasa.gov/diamond_jubilee/1996/sandage_hubble.html

Short Hubble Biography—
http://www.pbs.org/wgbh/aso/databank/entries/bahubb.html

Stephen Hawking's evaluation of Hubble—
http://www.pbs.org/wnet/hawking/cosmostar/html/hubble.html

Hubble Biography—
library.thinkquest.org/20230/people/edwinhub.htm?tqskip1=1&tqtime=o422

Glossary

astronomy - scientific study of the universe
atmosphere - layer of gases around a planet or star
bar exams - formal tests that an attorney must pass to practice law
Big Bang Theory - theory that the universe began about 15 billion years ago with a massive explosion and has continued expanding ever since
Cepheid - star that changes its degree of brightness at regular intervals
galaxy - very large group of stars held together by gravitational attraction
gravity - natural force that attracts objects to each other; the larger the objects, the greater the attraction
Hubble's Law - the fact that the farther away distant galaxies are, the faster they are moving away from the Earth
light-year - distance light travels in one year, about 5.9 trillion miles
magnitude - brightness of a star
Milky Way - spiral galaxy that contains our solar system
nebula - cloudy formation in space that may be clusters of stars, clouds of space dust, shells of gas around decaying stars or very distant galaxies
nova - star that suddenly increases in brightness due to exploding gases
observatory - building where astonomers use telescopes to study objects in space
phase - particular stage in a repeating cycle
red shift - indication that an object is moving away from the observer because light waves from the object are more spread out and appear redder
reflector telescope - telescope that uses a mirror to collect the light
refractor telescope - telescope that uses a glass lens to collect the light
solar system - sun and the objects that orbit it
spectroscopy - method of measuring the chemical composition of objects by passing rays of light from them through special gases
spectrum - pattern formed by light rays passed through gases; each element produces a different line pattern in its spectrum
star atlas - collection of maps and photographs of the night skies showing all known stars and other objects in space
velocity - speed at which an object travels

Index